T0055978

JOHN RUTTER

THE SPRIG OF THYME

A CYCLE OF FOLK-SONG SETTINGS
FOR MIXED CHOIR WITH CHAMBER ENSEMBLE
(OR CHAMBER ORCHESTRA)

MUSIC DEPARTMENT

OXFORD
UNIVERSITY PRESS

OXFORD
UNIVERSITY PRESS

Great Clarendon Street, Oxford OX2 6DP, England
198 Madison Avenue, New York, NY10016, USA

Oxford is a registered trademark of Oxford University Press

© Oxford University Press 1994

All rights reserved. No part of this publication may be reproduced, stored in a retrieval system, or transmitted, in any form or by any means, electronic, mechanical, photocopying, recording, or otherwise, without the prior permission in writing of Oxford University Press.

Permission to perform this work in public (except in the course of divine worship) should normally be obtained from the performing Right Society Ltd. (PRS), 29/33 Berners Street, London W1T 3AB, or its affiliated Societies in each country throughout the world, unless the owner or the occupier of the premises being used holds a licence from the society.

Permission to make a recording must be obtained in advance from the Mechanical Copyright Protection Society Ltd. (MCPS), Elgar House, 41 Streatham High Road, London SW16 1ER, or its affiliated Societies in each country throughout the world.

Instrumentation

Flute
Oboe
Clarinet in B flat and A
Bassoon
Harp
Violin 1
Violin 2
Viola
Cello
Bass

The string parts are intended for one player per part, but they can be doubled if the work is performed by chamber orchestra.

Instrumentation of the individual numbers is as follows:

Page		
1	1.	The bold grenadier: fl, ob, cl, bsn, hp, 2 vln, vla, vc, cb
5	2.	The keel row: fl, ob, cl, bsn
12	3.	The willow tree: hp, 2 vln, vla, vc, cb
16	4.	The sprig of thyme: 2 vln, vla, vc
19	5.	Down by the sally gardens: cl, 2 vln, vla, vc, cb
22	6.	The cuckoo: hp
29	7.	I know where I'm going: ob, 2 vln, vla, vc
32	8.	Willow song: unaccompanied
34	9.	O can ye sew cushions?: fl, hp, 2 vln, vla, vc, cb
37	10.	The miller of Dee: ob, cl, bsn
41	11.	Afton water: fl, ob, hp, 2 vln, vla, vc, cb

All performing material is available on hire from the publisher.

All eleven numbers from *The Sprig of Thyme* have been recorded by the Cambridge Singers and members of the City of London Sinfonia, directed by John Rutter, on the album *The Sprig of Thyme* (Collegium Records CD CSCD 517).

Duration: 35 minutes

Conductors may wish to select short groups of songs from *The Sprig of Thyme* for performance with specific instruments. For example, *The keel row* plus *The miller of Dee* requires only woodwind quartet; *The sprig of thyme* plus *I know where I'm going* requires oboe and string quartet; *The willow tree* plus *The cuckoo* requires harp and string quintet. *Willow song*, being unaccompanied, can be added to any selected group. (JR)

The sprig of thyme, *I know where I'm going*, and *O can ye sew cushions?* are also published together as *Three folk-songs for upper voices* (U167).
Down by the sally gardens and *The miller of Dee* are also published together as *Two folk-songs for male voices* (M23).

THE SPRIG OF THYME

arranged by
JOHN RUTTER

1. The bold grenadier

English folk-song

© Oxford University Press 1994

Printed in Great Britain
OXFORD UNIVERSITY PRESS, MUSIC DEPARTMENT, GREAT CLARENDON STREET, OXFORD OX2 6DP
Photocopying this copyright music is ILLEGAL.

25
A
TENORS and BASSES
mp
poco cresc.
bold gren - a - dier.
2. 'Good morn-ing, good morn-ing, good
32
mf
SOPRANOS and ALTOS mf
morn-ing,' said he: 'O_ where are you go - ing, my pret-ty la - dy?' 'I am go-ing a-
39
mp
walk - ing by the clear cry - stal stream, To see cool wa - ters glide and hear night-in - gales
p legato
B
45
(S. and A.) mf più animato
sing.
3. O sol-dier, O_ sol-dier, will you mar - ry
cresc.
mf
poco agitato

52
TENORS
and BASSES
mf
me?' 'Oh, no, my sweet la - dy, that ne-ver can be:
58
mp
For I've got a wife at home in my own coun - try; Two
dim.
p
64
wives and the ar - my's too ma - ny for me.'
dim.
Ped.
Ped.
71
C
S. and A.
unis.
p quasi lontano
As I was a - walk - ing one morn - ing in May, I spied a young cou - ple a -
T. and B.
unis.
p quasi lontano
pp
l.h.
Ped.

78
hay. O one was a fair maid and her beau - ty shone clear,
mak - ing of
hay. One fair beau - ty clear, And the
hay.
p
85
Hum
o - ther was a sol - dier, a bold gren - a - dier.
f
Ped.
*
90
mf
dim.
mp
rit.
dim.
p

2. The keel row

Northumbrian folk-song

21
B
I came thro' Sand-gate I heard a las-sie sing:
'O weel may the keel row, the keel row, the
mp
28
C
(mf)
keel row, O weel may the keel row that my lad-die's in. O weel may the
O weel
mf
34
keel row, the
keel row, the keel row, O weel may the keel row that my lad-die's
may the

D
40
unis.
mp
2. O who's like my John - ny, sae
in.
mf
mp
47
S.1
f
leish, sae blith, sae bon - ny, He's fore - most of the mo - ny keel lads o' coal - y Tyne.
S.2
+ A.
O
53
who's like my John - ny, sae leish, sae blith, sae bon - ny, He's fore - most of the mo - ny keel
Who
Fore - - most o' the
f
f

E
59
S.1
S.2
A.
T.
B.
S.1 and S.2
mf
leggiero
lads o' coal - y Tyne. He'll set and row so tight - ly, or in the dance so spright - ly, He'll
A.
mf leggiero
lads o' coal - y Tyne. He'll set and row so tight - ly, or in the dance so spright-ly,
lads o' Tyne.
lads o' Tyne.
mf
65
S.
A.
T.
B.
f
cut and shuf- fle sight - ly, 'tis true, were he not mine. He'll set and row so tight - ly, or
He'll cut and shuf- fle sight - ly, 'tis true, were he not mine. He'll set so tight - ly, or
He'll set and row so tight -
3

71
in the dance so spright - ly, He'll cut and shuf - fle sight - ly, 'tis true, were he not
in the dance so spright - ly, He'll cut and shuf - fle sight - ly, 'tis true, were he not
-ly, or in the dance so spright - ly, He'll cut so sight - ly, 'tis true, were he not
f
He'll cut and shuf - fle sight - ly, 'tis true, were he not
F
76
mine.
mine.
mine.
mine.
f
3
SOPRANOS
mp grazioso
82
3. He wears a blue bon - net, blue bon - net, blue bon - net, He
3
mp

89
G
f
wears a blue bon - net, a dim - ple in his chin.
He wears a blue bon - net, blue
f
3
f
95
mp
bon - net, blue bon - net, He wears a blue bon - net, a dim - ple in his chin. And
chin. And
mp
3
mp
101
weel may the keel row, the
weel may the keel row, the keel row, O weel may the keel row that

H
107
f
mf
my_ lad - die's in. O weel_ may the keel row, the keel_ row, the keel_ row, O
f
mf
f
dim.
I
113
p
weel_ may the keel_ row that_ my_
p
p
mf
p
121
lad - die's_ in.'
f
ff
Ped.
*

3. The willow tree

17
A
(Hum)
die be - neath the wil - low tree.
cresc.
mf
espress.
22
mp
mf
mp
mf
Ped.
B
29
unis.
mf
2. My love hath wealth and beau - ty, rich_ suit-ors at - tend her door, My___ love hath wealth and
unis.
mf
sim.

35
(mf) dolce
beau-ty, she slights me be-cause I'm poor. The rib-bon fair that bound her hair is
(mf) dolce
40
mp
3
C
all that is left to me, While here I lie a-lone to die be-neath the wil-low tree.
mp
p
46
p
Hum
unis. p
3. I once had gold and sil-ver, I thought them with-
mp
p

52
(Hum)
TENORS only
mp
- out end, I once had gold and sil - ver, I thought I had a true friend. My
D
(TENORS)
57
wealth is lost, my friend is false, my love hath he sto - len from me, While
sim.
rall. al fine
61
p
dim.
pp
here I lie a - lone to die be - neath the wil - low tree.
pp
Ped.
*

4. The sprig of thyme

(*sopranos only*)

22
stand - ing by: I bade him choose for me. He chose me the
29
mp
li - ly and the vio - let and the pink But these I re - fused all three.
p
B
36
mp dolce
3. Thyme it is the pret - ti - est thing, And time it will grow on,
43
// p
And time it will bring all things to an end, And so does my
//
pp

50
f
C
mf
time grow on. 4. It's ve - ry well drink - ing ale, And it's
f
mf
Poco meno mosso
56
mp
ve - ry well drink - ing wine: But it's far bet - ter sit - ting by a
mp
rit.
62
p
young man's side That has won this heart of mine.
3
p

5. Down by the sally gardens

(*tenors and basses*)

Words by W. B. YEATS

Irish traditional melody

15
p
bid me_ take love ea - sy, As the leaves grow on_ the_ tree. But I be-ing young and
mp
dim.
p
20
fool - ish, With her did_ not a-gree.
25
mp
2. In a field_____ by the_ ri - - ver My_ love and_ I did
mp
29
stand._____ And on my_ lean - ing_ shoul - der She_ placed her_ snow - white

33
dim.
hand. She bid me take life ea - sy, As the grass grows on the
37
p
mp
p
poco rit.
weirs. But I was young and fool - ish, And now am full of
p
mp
p
a tempo
rall.
41
pp
tears.
pp

6. The cuckoo

English folk-song

A
18
mp
cuc - koo, the sum - mer draw - eth near.
2. As
2nd SOPRANOS
p
ALTOS
Hum
TENORS
BASSES
p
A
24
I was a - walk - ing and a - talk - ing one day, I met my own true love, as

30
B
cresc.
mf
he came that_ way. O to meet him was a plea - sure, tho' the court - ing was a
mp Aw
Aw
Aw
mp Aw
B
35
3
woe, For I found him_ false - heart - ed,_ he would kiss_ me and go._
mf

Tempo rubato
rit.
a tempo
C
40
SOPRANOS 1 and 2
p legato
ALTOS
3. I wish I were a
3. I were a
p legato
Tempo rubato
rit.
a tempo
C
f
dim.
p
46
mp
scho - lar
p
and could han - dle the per. I would write to my lov - er and to all rov - ing
scho - lar
mp
I would tell them of the grief and woe that at - tend on their
52
mf
cresc.
men.
mf
I would tell, that at - tend on their
men.
that at - tend
mf
mf
cresc.
men.
I would tell of grief and of all their

56
f
mf
dim.
lies, I would wish them have pi - ty on the flow - er when it
60
mp dim.
pp
D
dies.
dies, when it dies.
dies,
dies.
p
64
1st SOPRANOS or SOLO
p lontano
O the cuc - koo she's a pret - ty bird, she

67
sing - eth as she flies; She
70
bring - eth good ti - dings, she tell - eth no
73
S.
lies.
1st and 2nd
SOPRANOS
p
Mm
A.
p
Ah
dim.
T.
B.
p
Ah
dim.

76
dim.
pp
Mm

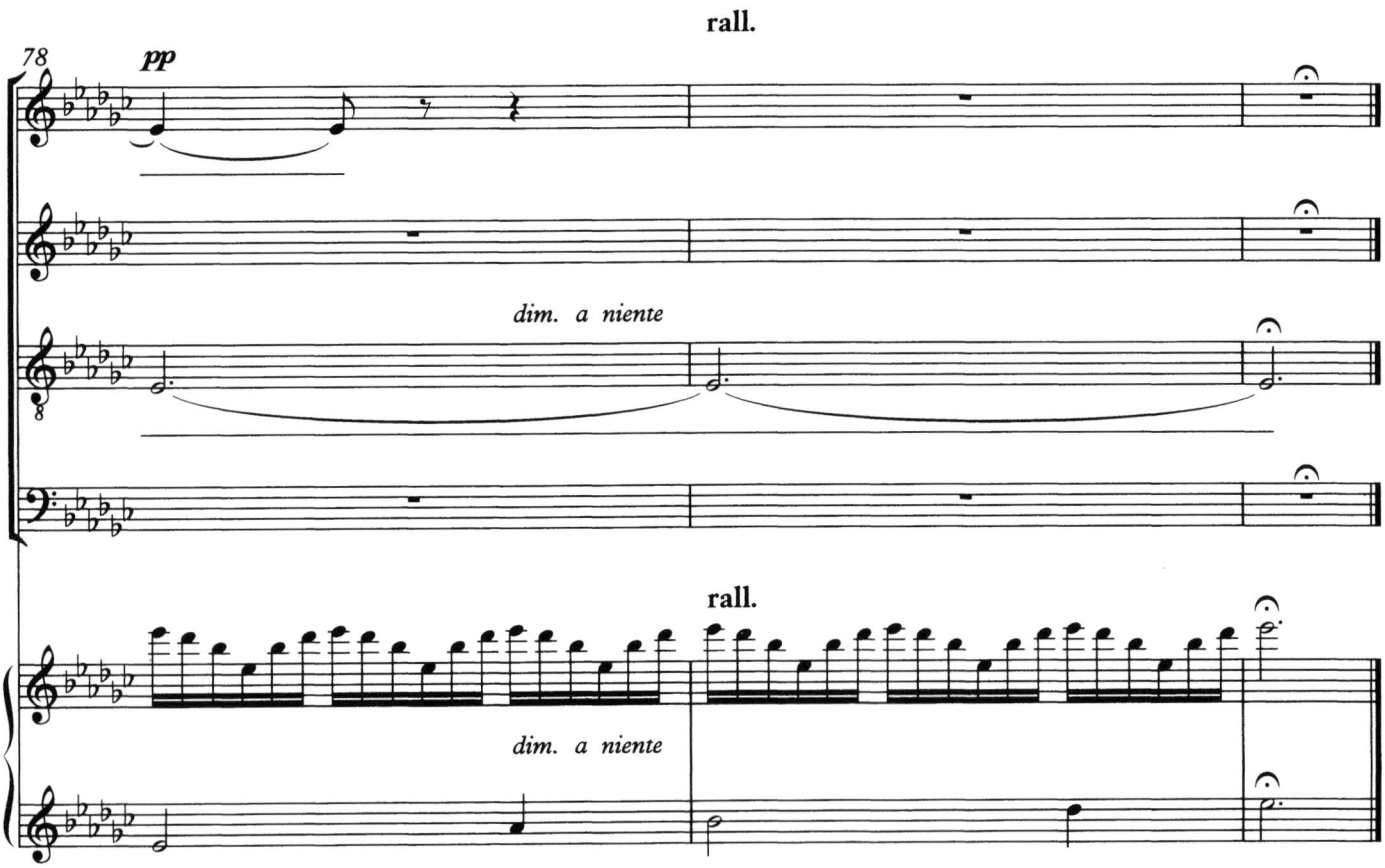
rall.
78
pp
dim. a niente
rall.
dim. a niente

7. I know where I'm going

(*sopranos only*)

Irish folk-song

21
mf
mp
Shoes of fine green lea-ther, Combs to buck-le my hair, And a ring for ev-'ry fin-ger.
mf
mp
27
C
mp
mf
3. Some say he's black,
p
mp
mf
36
mp
But I say he's bon-ny, The fair-est of them all My hand-some, win-some
mp
43
D
pp
John-ny.
4. Fea-ther beds are
mf
pp

50
p
mp
soft, And paint - ed rooms are bon - ny, But I would leave them all— To— go with my love
mp
56
E
p
John - ny.
I know where I'm go - ing,— And
mf
p
Meno mosso
63
mp
p
dim.
a niente
I know who's going with me, I know who I love— But the dear knows who I'll mar - ry.
mp
p
dim. a niente

8. Willow song

(A poor soul sat sighing)

16th-century melody and words

25
p
(p)
wil - low!
Mm
Sing wil - low, wil-low, wil-low!
2. He sighed in his sing-ing and made a great moan,
I am
mp
mp
p
Mm
p
wil-low!
Mm
O wil-low, wil-low, wil-low, wil-low, O
32
mp
Mm
O wil - - low, wil-low, O
dead to all plea-sure, my true love is gone! O wil-low, wil-low, wil-low, wil - low, O
mf
dim.
mp
p
mp
Mm
O wil - - - - low, O
38
dim.
p
pp
wil-low, wil-low, wil-low, wil - low
My gar - land shall be. Sing all a green wil-low,
wil - - low, wil - low
wil - - - - low
dim.
p
pp
44
wil - low, wil-low, wil-low, Ah me! the green wil - low my gar - land must be.
gar - land

9. O can ye sew cushions?

(sopranos and altos)

Scottish folk-song

23
hee and baw lamb, And hee and baw bird - ie, my bon - ny wee lamb.
31
mp
B
2. I placed my cra - dle On yon hol - ly top, And ay as the
mp
38
p
wind blew My cra - dle did rock. And hush - a - baw bird - ie, and ba - li - lee
p
44
loo, And hee and baw bird - ie, my bon - ny wee doo.

C
52
espress.
p
Ped.
*
60
pp molto dolce
And hee and baw bird - ie, and hee and baw lamb, And hee and baw
pp
67
rit.
bird - ie, my bon - ny wee lamb.
Ped.
*

10. The miller of Dee

(*tenors and basses*)

17
A
care for no - bo-dy, no, not I, If no - bo-dy cares for me.
f
mf
22
mf
2. I
mp
mf
mp
26
love my mill, she is to me Both pa - rent, child and wife.
I
30
f
would not change my sta - tion for An - o - ther one in life.
Then

B
34
mf
push, push, push the bowl, my boys, And pass it round to me; The
f
38
C
lon - ger we sit here and drink, The mer - ri - er we shall be.'
mf
f
43
TENORS
f
3. Then like the mill - er bold and free Let
BASSES
f
3. Then like the mill - er bold and free Let
sf
mf
f

48
us re - joice and sing. The days of youth were made for glee, And
us re - joice and sing. The days of youth were made for glee, And time is on the
mf
53
D
unis.
time is on the wing. This song shall pass A - round this jo - vial
wing. This song shall pass from me to thee A - round this jo - vial
f
Largamente
rall.
58
cresc.
ff
ring: Let heart and voice and all a - gree To sing 'Long live the King!'
ring: Let heart and voice and all a - gree To sing 'Long live the King!'
cresc.
ff

11. Afton water

Scottish folk-song

13
Af - ton, a - mong thy green braes, Flow gen - tly, I'll sing thee a song in thy
19
TENORS
mp
praise. My Ma - ry's a - sleep by thy mur-mur - ing stream, Flow gen - tly, sweet
SOPRANOS
and TENORS
p
25
Af - ton, dis - turb not her dream.
A
A
mp
dolce
Ped.
Ped.

30
p
Aw
Aw
TENORS and BASSES unis.
mp
2. How loft - y, sweet Af - ton, thy neigh-bour-ing hills, Far marked with the
dim.
sim.
p
36
mp
There dai - ly I wan-der as dawn ri - ses
cours-es of clear wind-ing rills.
42
p
high, My flocks and my Ma - ry's sweet cot in my eye.
p
mp

48
B
p dolce e legato
3. How plea - sant thy banks and green val - leys be - low, Where
p dolce e legato
B
pp
54
wild in the wood - lands the prim - ro - ses blow! There oft as mild
59
eve - ning creeps o - ver the lea, The sweet scent - ed birk shades my Ma - ry and

65
me.
pp
p dolce
con Ped.
71
unis.
pp
C
4. Flow gen - tly, sweet Af - ton, a - mong thy green braes, Flow
unis.
pp
C
pp
Ped.
*
76
p
gen - tly, sweet ri - ver, the theme of my lays. My Ma - ry's a -
p

Printed in England by Caligraving Limited Thetford Norfolk